VOLUME I

BY
REA-SILVIA COSTIN, P.E.

Copyright © 2024 Rea-Silvia Costin, P.E.

All rights reserved

About me

The need to write came into my life unexpectedly and with such force that it left me no choice but to follow.

I published my first book *Short Stories: The Story of a Refugee* with Vantage Press in 1997. In 2003, I published the first book of a trilogy, *ThianaAVDELA-A Macedonian Village in the Northwestern Greece: Thiana's Native Land* and in 2004, I published the second volume of the trilogy *ATHENS* with iUniverse. American Publishing Company has published the third book of the trilogy *America - The Final Destination.*

My poetry is published in *The Best Poems and Poets of 2001, 2002, 2003,* and 2005, *The Theatre of the Mind,* and *The Celebrations of Honors* as well as *Who's Who in Poetry 2004 and 2005,* editions by the International Library of Poetry. In May 2002, I obtained my Laureate Certificate from the International Library of Poets. I am the recipient of the Editor's Choice Award, 2002, 2003, 2005, from the poetry.com site as well as the President's Award for Excellence in Literature from the National Authors Registry.

In January 2005, I joined the Poets.com Workshop under the pen name of Frantzi500 (my nickname). I include in this book a poem that I cherish and which was dedicated to my poetry and me, authored by Lynnewood Jeffrey Shafer I (Godbreathed) of poets. com.

I was born in Greece and raised in Romania. I am a Professional Engineer.

What does poetry mean to me?It's a way to express deep feel-ings, to share with others my philosophy and understanding of life, and to give testimony of my faith in God.

Table of Contents

You

To Frantzi500 and all the other wonderful Poets who I wish to Tag.
You,
have made
me smile;
that turned
to tears;
you made
me care.

To know your pain
I touched your shame;
to see those eyes
that feel the same.

The ink still wet,
with hearts regret
of words that pry
to ask you why.

Of love and pain while hope remains;
these words that live
from hearts who give.

You,
have made
me sing;
of songs
way deep;
where rivers spring.

As calmness flows
and reasons grow;
where words and heart
our oneness knows.
You,
have made

me cry;
of pain
you feel;
that flood my eyes.

And sorrows hold
of times not told;
for pen and heart
a soul unfold.

You,
have made
me smile;
have made
me sing;
have made

me cry.

Lynnewood Jeffrey Shafer I.
by <u>odbreathed</u>

Author's Comments:
"The common inspiration that binds Poets together, is the heart, and the issues that flow from within. Your impact is not primarily in your words, but rather your heart. The pen that dips into the inkwell of the heart, has an endless supply from which to write...Too you, I write this poem. You have all left an unmistakable fine impression..Frantzi500, you are the inspiration for this poem.. God bless you." Lynnewood Jeffrey Shafer I.

Pearls on a String.

Unforgettable memories
That form the songs of one's life,
Beautiful pearls on a golden string.

I cherish mine;
Often look at them,
With my mind's eye;
And a window opens
In my soul;
The happiness that once was,
Invade my being.

Once more,
Making me wish,
For more
Unforgettable memories!

Rea-Silvia Costin, P.E. © 2005.

I Long...

I long to grow wings
that I could shed the old me,
the me that is shy, and modest, and careful.

I long that overnight,
I transform from a caterpillar
into a butterfly with bright, colorful wings,
carelessly flying into sunshine.
I long to leave my leaden shoes
that keep me grounded to the earth
and soar as an eagle.

I long that for once,
I might love with no fear, and no boundaries.

I long that for once,
I could rip the mask from my face
and reveal to the world the real me,
as I am inside, the beautiful butterfly, instead of the caterpillar
that people see looking at me.

I long that for once,

I live as if I really liked myself.

Rea-Silvia Costin, P.E. © 2005

Author's Comments:
This poem is posted on my poetry.com web site under my name and was published by Noble House in "The Theatre of the Mind" collection.

My Place of Origin

I'm so confused:
Where is my place of origin?

Is it Greece, Thessaloniki?
The town in the northwestern Greece
Where I was born?
Cannot remember it,
But from my mother's stories,
From my grandmother's dialect,

Or maybe Bucharest, Romania,
The place I grew up?
My father's beloved country
With its rich traditions,
Focsani, Moldova and the relatives
From my father's side,
The slow, soft speaking people,
The monasteries,
That I visited as a child,
The rich cuisine,
The wine country,
The Carpathian Mountains

That I hiked as a teenager,
The Black Sea seashore and its outlying regions
That I enjoyed as a young adult.

Then back to Greece and Athens
The ancient city,
With its old architecture,
And the beautiful
Topaz Mediterranean Sea.

Or Florida, my new county
With its beautiful shores and
Marshes
With the Walt Disney attractions
And my new house and job,
My new life
So what is my origin?
I'm confused.

Rea-Silvia Costin, P.E. © 2005

Poetry

It all started unexpectedly, at a writer's workshop.

I had never written poetry before,
never dreamed I could.

It was the unreachable dream,
a gift to the few chosen.

When the instructor,
a gifted poet herself,
encouraged us to put our thoughts on paper,
they came out as a poem.

Tangled feelings,
strong emotions,
pain, love,
frustration, jealousy,
sadness, loss,
tightly bottled inside,
for so long,
became untangled on paper,
like a clear stream of coherent words.

What a better way of freeing yourself
of the burden of emotions
overwhelming emotions,
but to put them on the paper,
as a poem!

Rea-Silvia Costin, P.E.©2005

Author's Comments:
This poem was published in "The Best Poems and Poets of 2001" and was awarded the Editor's Choice Award.

Grace

The Grace of God is pouring over you,
from Above,
like a shower of spring rain,
like a stream of light.
The Grace of God is entering your being,
engulfing you.
Then, and only then, you can sit at your computer,
and write the word of God,
which is poured into you from above.
You're just an instrument,
a chosen person to write down
the word of God onto the paper.
Two hands typing away at the computer keys.
Your vanity is hollow,
it's not you writing the verses on the paper,
it's not you typing the words on the keyboard,
It's the Grace of God,

enfolding you
like a mantle of sunrays.

Rea-Silvia Costin, P.E.©2005

To Father

In the memory of my beloved father

I stopped in the doorway, looking at you;
You seemed so frail, in your green, velvet coat.
The month was June, but you still wore
The coat that we bought you at Christmas.
You were seated at the square, oak table
Next to the window, your observation point.
In front of you was a makeshift calendar
And you scratched the days off, as they passed.
I walked into the room and sat at the table
Across from you, to look at your beloved face,
Perhaps for the last time.
I was on my way out to better and greater places,
To build a future for you and myself.
You looked at me, your kind eyes magnified by the reading glasses,
"My little girl, Go!" you said.
You knew then that we would not meet again.
Father, you were wrong!

Because you live within me
Within my heart, within my soul, within my mind!

Rea-Silvia Costin, P.E.

Copyright ©2005 Rea-Silvia Costin

Author's Comments:
This poem was selected for publication into "Who's Who in Poetry 2005"
Anthology.

Bucharest

To: Bucharest, the City where I grew up.

Twenty long years passed,
Finally, finally, I went back Home,
to Romania! What a change
in the place, in the people, in the air,
in my beloved City, Bucharest!

First day, coming back from America,
the big city, breathing,
in and out like a giant, seemed dirty;
The old architectural buildings gray
with fumes, the streets trashy.

Few days into my stay, I start looking
back at the monumental buildings
with fondness, and rediscovered
the wonders of the architecture,
the majestic lines, the attention
to the details. The dirt did not seem
to bother me any longer…

I walked and walked until my feet
had blisters, I had to visit the old
School "Sava" that I attended, the garden,
Cismigiu, in the middle of town.
I had to walk along Calea Victoriei,
the main street, as so many times before.

And near the towns' center my home…
My beloved home, where I grew up
my home, that they transformed
into a factory after I left….

I rode the metro, the marvelous subway
system, that was built in my absence
I visited the Union Square
with its white, unfinished palaces
reminding of the former Dictator.

I basked bumping into the milling
people on the streets, feeling myself once again
a part of a living organism.

Rea-Silvia Costin, P.E.@2005

Child of God

I knew I was a child of God ever
Since, as a small child, I listened to
My father's spare teachings of the Bible;
The seed fell on fertile ground
Took strong roots and grew.

I knew I was a child of God
When as a teenager I learned
The theory of Darwinism in School.
My faith was not shaken
By the communist teachings and religious restrictions.

In my heart and soul
There was a light, a love, warmth,
A security that none could take away,
Even if I did not attend church,
Or wasn't schooled in bible teachings,
I knew I was God's child.

When life's adversities
Blew as a strong storm over my family,
I was the cornerstone

Calm, my faith strong
I knew that God would bring us safe to shore.

When I defected from my country
And traveled to Greece and then to America, alone,
I knew I wasn't alone,
For God carried me in the palm of his hand to safe harbor,
And helped me bring the family over, for safe harbor.

When devil's creatures tried to take
Away from me the fruits of my work,
Which I saw in tears and sweat
God was there protecting me.
I could feel his love like a warm blanket, snug around me.

God, this world is yours
Keep it safe, keep your people safe
Bring peace to the world,
Bring love to the world,
Keep us safe, in the palm of your hand.

Rea-Silvia Costin, P.E. @2005

God's Mansion.

I'll never get back there.
I'll never put my foot inside that house.
Somebody else has it now.
The high ceilings, the paint and moldings,
Different colors in each room,
Green, blue, beige, and red,
Matching the colors of the tall, ceramic stoves,
The sun filtering through heavy, velvet drapes,
Different colors in each room,
Matching the colors of the antique, ceramic stoves
The gleaming of the hard wood floors,
The tall, white doors with intricate moldings on top,
Painted in different colors in each room
Matching the color of the corner ceramic stoves.
The feeling that I'm home…
"You're home," the voice at the end of the tunnel said
"God has a mansion for you in heaven,

You're home now!"

Rea-Silvia Costin, P.E.© 2005

Author's Comments:
I wrote this poem about the house I grew up in back in Romania, that the government took over when we left the country to immigrate to the USA.

Christmas Morning

A doll's carriage
Was all I could think of
Was all I could dream of
That was my desire for Christmas.

Three-years-old, I knew exactly
What I wanted and expected Santa to bring
On Christmas morning
Under the tall tree.

Wise beyond my years,
One will say, even at the young age of three
I could not take any chances
I had to devise a back up plan, just in case....

So, in the weeks before the big holiday
Nestling in bed next to mother at naptime
I could get her ear and made sure she knew
What my heart's desire was.

Not much did I sleep
The Christmas night,

My hopes high
That my dreams would be fulfilled.

In the big, frigid room; it was really a ballroom
Hardly used in winter times,
Where the Christmas tree reached the high ceiling
And under the tree, the presents for us, the children

I went and started to unwrap all of them randomly
Looking for mine
A wooden train with its red wagons
That's for my little brother Radu
I thought and tossed it on side
Another big package;
I ripped the paper off

A doll's bed, nicely finished
With blue velvet
It might be for my sister, Mady
Because that's not what I wanted

And then I saw it!
It was soo big that it could not be wrapped properly
A real carriage for my doll
It was light blue, made of wood
With soft flowery cushions

I screamed with delight
And tuning around
I dragged the carriage in full circle
Around the ornate Christmas tree.

Santa and mother worked wonders!

Rea-Silvia Costin, P.E.©2005

Idle Conversation

"Don't be greedy,
you don't need another house here!"
"Why not?"
"You're going to lose the house up there!"
"Where?"
"You know where, up there,
the house that GOD is preparing for you."
"Is God preparing a house for me?"
"Yes!"
"Where?"
"Up there, you know, with Him.
That's why we're here, now,
so God can prepare our mansion over there!"

Rea-Silvia Costin, P.E.©2005

Author's Comments:
*This poem is also posted on the poetry.com web site under my real
name and was selected for inclusion on the "Sound of Poetry."*

Athens

To the country where I was born: Greece.
Greece, Athens
I can't open that door yet.
I shut it closed and I can't open it now.
Me crying on the streets of Athens
Openly, in the middle of the day
The unmistaken feeling
That's where I belong.
How true it is
The saying That where you were born
That's where you belong.
Athens in summer,
The beaches, my relatives there...
The freedom to walk on the streets,
The freedom to be alone,
The fullness and emptiness of being alone.

Rea-Silvia Costin, P.E.©2005

Easter

For all of those of Eastern and Greek Orthodox faith: Christ is risen!

Greece, at Easter time...
A few years back,
like in another lifetime.
A small, white village, in the mountains,
The evening of Good Friday....
Dark outside,
Candles in hand, we went to the church,
a small building,
nestled among the rocks.
The entire village outside, waiting....
The funeral of our Lord
The deacons carried the epitaphion outside,
gilded wood overlaid with gold,
that women's loving hands
covered in flowers.
It stopped in the middle of the village
The night was cold and clear...
Deafening silence,
bowed heads,
lighted candles,

Nature withholding its breath,
Only the clear voice of the priest chanting
The lighted stars watching from above,
weeping, the death of our Lord,
Jesus Christ.

Rea-Silvia Costin, P.E.© 2005

Author's Comments:
*This poem is also posted on my web site at poetry.com and was published
into "The Celebration of Honor" by Cedar Press. For this poem I was
awarded the National Authors' Award for Literature Excellency.*

Budding Rose

His hands, tightly cupped
Over the caps of his knees
As he stood, hunched over, watching her… His big hands tightly
cupped as if
With the roundness of her face
His knuckles white with restraint… The young girl in front of him
Inviting,
Ready to open for love
Like a spring bud ready to unravel its petals
Pure, untamed
Innocent…
Should he dare
Even touch her?
Even thinking about loving her?
She was only a child to him,
Lovely and smart.
His heart aching,
Beating fast at the gate of his chest
His big hands full with the fullness of her cheeks
His knuckles white with restraint…
He wouldn't dare touch
The innocent, beautiful girl in front of him,

And mar the budding flower
And its delicate petals.

Rea-Silvia Costin ©2002

Falling in Love

Falling in love,
The Utopia and
Euphoria of it all.
Yet, without love
There is no life,
Just empty time
Passing you by.

Rea-Silvia Costin, P.E.© 2005

High on the Cliff

To a lost Love.

Night, full moon
The sea splashing against rocks,
Furious, dark
Somewhere, nearby,
Lights, laughs, life, and joy

Two lovers,
Cuddled against each other,
High on the cliff,
Down, the sea foaming
White, like a thick cloud,

Silver moonlight, outshaping their bodies,
Kisses like living water, satiating the souls
Bodies intertwined, like limbs in a jungle,
Hands clasped together,
As if, to hold onto each other forever.

They did not know
Forever
is as short as
Tomorrow.

Rea-Silvia Costin, P.E. © 2005

Chemistry of the Hearts

Love...
What is it all about?
The right chemistry of the bodies?
The right chemistry of the minds?
Or, the right chemistry of the hearts?
Or maybe all of the above...
What's the right answer?
What is one to search for?
All of the above...
The chemistry of the souls intertwined,
Hand in hand,
Heads bending toward one another,
Bodies touching, minds stretching
their understanding,
Souls and hearts opening doors,
Intertwining...
What is love?
An overall feeling of well being,

A completion, peace, fulfillment
All of the above and more, so much more...
Rea-Silvia Costin, P.E.

Copyright ©2005 Rea-Silvia Costin, P.E.

Perfect Love Casts Out All Fear

Perfect love casts out all fear
It casts out all demons
Jesus' love is perfect
To love again,
To trust again,
Completely,
To get close
To another person again,
Intimately close,
Fears have to be cast out
Fear of
Rejection,
Hurt,
Commitment

Let Jesus' love cleanse your heart
Make it whole again
Open up the doors
For

Love
Trust
Commitment

Perfect love cast out all fears
Let it happen, let it happen!

Rea-Silvia Costin, P.E. ©2005

The Dream

The other night, I had a dream,
One of those nightmares
That I have not deciphered yet,
Try as I may.

As if two birds were inside my home,
One, a peacock, with turquoise spotted tail
And a small tiara on her head
As a bride with its bejeweled train,
Gentle and meek, peace loving.

The other, a crow,
A large bird with clipped, black feathers
Loud and snappy, curt
A dark shadow of the fair one.

They were keeping close company,
The fair and the black,
Both hungry, both waiting to be fed.

The fair one, I loved to look upon
The black one, I feared, as a black omen

Try as I may to separate them
I could not, the two faces of the same mask.

Rea-Silvia Costin

Copyright ©2005 Rea-Silvia Costin

Author's Comments:
This poem was published into the 2002 collection of "Poets Laureate."

Your Enemy

Your enemy is trying to build walls around you
Your enemy is trying to nail you in a casket
together with a crazy person
Your enemy is trying to squeeze the life out of you, drop by drop
Precious drop after precious drop
Don't let it happen, fight back!
Ask the other person what he meant
Ask him immediately
Before the wall is built around you
The tall, stone wall
The cold wall isolating you from the warmth of others
From the sunshine . . . from love
Ask him what he meant when he hurt you with his cruel words
Don't let the wall build around you
Isolating you from the one you love
Ask him what he meant by his unthoughtful words
That he hurtled at you

Don't let the cold, stone wall rise between you
Fight back
And your enemy will flee you.
Rea-Silvia Costin

Copyright ©2005 Rea-Silvia Costin

Author's Comments:
This poem was published into the "Colors of the Past" anthology by the International Library of Poetry.

Everlasting Love

God loves you with an everlasting
Love
because is the only hope for this sick world
God has blessed you with the power of
Love
for is God's solution to a sick world

Love
overpowers greed,
and hate,
and meanness

Love heals wounds,
and broken hearts,
soothes and mends
where hate has spread destruction...

Love,
open your door to me again,

replace the coldness and aloofness
from my heart,
mend my broken heart,
sooth my very soul,
that I can share God's Love
with others again.

Rea-Silvia Costin, P.E. © 2005

The Intruder

I pressed my face to the wrought-iron gate
even before I bought my entrance ticket
to the amusement park.
Avidly, I searched the crowd for him. . . .
Finally, I spotted him, like an overgrown boy,
dressed in his blue swimsuit,
a huge orange inner tube in hand,
climbing the steps to the highest flume
and sliding down the water slide
among the children
splashing into the pool
at the toe of the flume.
Grinning, eyes closed, limbs sprawled,
then seizing the tube again
and climbing the stairs
waiting for the next marvelous experience.
Happily, I shouted out his name.
He turned, looked with myopic eyes toward me.

Suddenly, I realized I had spoiled his fun;
I was the intruder.

Rea-Silvia Costin ©2005

Sunset

Sunset,
The sun, a globe of fire,
Incandescent,
Falling into the ocean

On the deserted beach,
Two lovers
Tormented with desire

The man persuaded his mate
On the white sand
Covering Her
With delicious kisses

The warm water selected
The color of the sunset
Red- gold

The two lovers comparing
Suntans

Their bodies tarnished
Like bronzes
Intertwined.

Rea-Silvia Costin, P.E. © 2005

The Forbidden Fruit

I drank from the forbidden fountain,
I ate from the forbidden tree
The fountain of love,
The tree of knowledge

Oh! How foolish,
How foolish of me!
I tasted the sweetness
of the forbidden fruit,
the forbidden love…

Stolen moments of happiness
that belonged to somebody else
Happiness? No. Not really!
Just ecstasy, dizziness, a thick fog
Overcoming senses

Love, the forbidden fruit
How sweet, yet how bitter.

Rea-Silvia Costin, P.E. © 2005

Jealousy is a Horse The Devil Likes to Ride

The gripping hands of jealousy,
The ripping pain,
The flames of hell burning up your soul,
The grip of death tightening around your heart...

Jealousy, the most destructive weapon,
It destroys love,
It destroys friendship,
It destroys houses
It destroys oneself...

Jealousy, the most cruel weapon,
That the devil devised,
And takes pleasure from using it
Upon innocent victims,
The victims who opened their hearts
To love,
To happiness,
The most vulnerable ones.

Just say NO to the devil,
And his weapons will fail to work
Their deadly grip upon you!

Rea-Silvia Costin, P.E.©2005

Let Your Guard Down.

Let down your guard,
Break down the barriers,
Carefully erected around your heart,
The walls which protect you from hurting,
Ever again.

Let down your guard
For the waves of love
To wash over your heart again.
The love you so desire,
To flood your heart again.

Let your guard down,
That the sweet love
May reach your heart again,
And flood your whole being
With the sweetness of it.

Rea-Silvia Costin, P.E.©2005

Your Faith Gives Me Strength.

Your faith gives me strength,
To grow spiritually,
To reach highs, I know,
I couldn't climb on my own

Your faith inspires me
To write poetry, to express
Feelings inside me,
To reveal my soul's bareness

Your faith funnels,
A direct line of communication
For the Holy Spirit
To use me as his extension

Your faith is the candle
Lighting in the night
In front of me
To show me the path,
The narrow and straight one

Your faith made me realize
The wrongful ways,
The path to sin and destruction
Your faith brought me back
To the straight and narrow one

Your faith brought me
Closer to God, and to you
Our shared faith made us,
Grow spiritually

Our shared faith
Teaches us the way,
To shared Love,
Understanding,
Peace.

Rea-Silvia Costin, P.E. ©2005.

Make Me Whole.

Oh, how I wished,
time and time again, for your love...
Oh, how I wished,
that once your heart touched mine,
as so many times before,
to leave it there, with mine...
Oh, how many times I wished,
the grueling search to end,
two hearts to become one,
instead of two incomplete halves,
traveling time alone,
searching for one another...
Oh, it's so much peace and sweetness,
so much comfort, and happiness,
when two hearts became a whole
finally together, the search over,
two souls intertwined
traveling time, traveling eternity.
Oh, leave your heart with mine,

Make me whole, make me whole!

Rea-Silvia Costin

Copyright ©2005 Rea-Silvia Costin

The Heart on a String

Once upon a time,
I read a children's story.
It was a Russian story
about a little boy
who had a dog.
The little boy used to tie
a piece of meat to a string,
and tricked the little dog to eat it,
only to pull the piece of meat out
by its string, once the little dog ate it.

The boy loved the dog,
it was his playmate, it was his best friend.

Today, I remember the story
of the little boy and his dog
as I'm thinking of you,
and how you're playing with my heart,
the same cruel play.
You're giving me a bit of love,
the sweet love I crave so,
only to pull it back by its string

once the love has reached my heart.

The boy loved the dog,
it was his playmate, it was his best friend.

Rea-Silvia Costin, P.E.© 2005

Author's Comments:
This poem is also posted on my web site at poetry.com under my real name and was published by the Noble House in its collection "Colours of the Heart."

Conversation among Angels

Like an outsider seeking the warmth of a lighted house
On a cold, brisk night
A young woman is kneeling
In front of a locked door
With a handful of keys in her hand
Trying one key after the other patiently
Trying to unlock the door
That she'd like so much to open
For years, without success.
Her patience is waning short…
"That door opens only from inside;
She does not know it though,"
The first Angel whispers.
"Tell her that!
Tell her that the door opens only from inside!
At least, she would be able to rest,"
The second Angel said.
"I'm waiting for her to ask me
To ask for my help

Then, and only then
Will I help her open the door
The door to love and warmth
The door to the house
She's so longing to get inside."

Rea-Silvia Costin, P.E. ©2005

Rivalry

I dream of her
and her evil works;
like the worm webs,
tightly woven around the limbs
of a young bough;
white, sticky,
suffocating the bough;
the young bough dying,
under her evil spell.

Brushing the web aside
from the dead limbs,
suddenly, I saw a young limb,
fresh, and a bud
ready to open and spring to life.

There is life there,
there is still love;

The dried bough
will spring back to life
Her evil works dispel
she did not win after all!

Rea-Silvia Costin ©2002

I Won

I won the battle;
The battle I was carrying on with the enemy;
With myself,
I won the battle against jealousy and greed.
Against ugliness.
I'm free!
People had mistreated me,
And poked fun at me;
And I, for the first time,
Have not reacted as they expected:
Tooth for tooth and nail for nail,
Ugliness for ugliness;
For the first time, I succeeded to rise above it all,
And be myself,
Clean, pure at heart.
I succeeded in controlling the gates to my soul,
To stop the ugliness from getting inside,
And becoming part of me.

I raised above it all,
And the love of God filled my soul,
With joy, with light.
I won the battle;
Will I be able to win the war?

Rea-Silvia Costin ©2000

Unshared Love

Unshared love,
Rejection,
One-sided love,
It's the living hell.

Soon it will destroy your heart,
Will destroy your self-esteem,
Will erode your sanity, and will deem you worthless,
Will reduce you to nothing more than a doormat

I know it, because
I have been there!
Get out of it
While you still can!

Rea-Silvia Costin, P.E. ©2005

If Nobody Loves Me.

If nobody loves me,
If everybody turns his or her back on me,
If I ever be left alone,
To face harsh adversities,
I'm still not alone;
The Lord loves me.

If people tell me
That I don't measure up,
That I'm not as beautiful
As other women are,
That I'm not as intelligent as other people are,
That I'm not as sweet as other girls are,
I have to remember:
God still loves me,
Just the way I am,
Uniquely made
In His perfect image.

If nobody loves me,
The Lord still does;
I'm his beloved child
Made uniquely in his likeliness,
Perfect, just as I am.

@ Rea-Silvia Costin, P.E. © 2005

Phoenix

When God closes one door
He will open another one
For sure.

The door He closed today
Was long due to being closed.
Regardless, the pain with which it squeezed my heart
With its closing movement
Is hard to bear…

It closed with a thunder
As thrown by an angry hand
The brusque movement caught my heart within
And the heavy door closed on it.

God will open a new door, for sure.
As you have to discard old clothes to make room for new ones,
That's how the old heart needs to be burned
And from the ashes a new love to emerge.

Rea-Silvia Costin© 2001

Repentance

I kneel to the ground, my head bowed down
I'm humbling myself in front of the Lord
Asking for the remission of my sins

I have paid the price, a high price indeed, for all my sins
I have suffered and cried, tears of blood
I have wasted my life, the better part of it
I have wasted God's gift to me,
The children I never had, and so much wanted

I have paid a high price
For an hour of stolen happiness, for a crumb of love
I have paid the price without complaining
Knowing that I have sinned, and that I deserve to pay for it,

But I never repented; not really; not in my heart
There were excuses for my behavior; other people's faults
Now, I repent
Now, I understand that I sold myself and the living God inside me,
Short, for a crumb of love

I so much wanted love that I settled for a crumb, a pitiful crumb
Instead of waiting for the feast planned for me by the Lord
And by doing so I sold myself short of the glory of God

Rea-Silvia Costin ©2000

To Mother: The Sacred Gift of Life

In loving memory of my Mother.

Sucking air through the oxygen mask
tightly bounded around your small, dear face.
Your mouth opens, sucking the air, the life.
Like a little fish out of the water,
opening its little mouth, trying to breathe.
"I'm O.K.," you answered happily,
your open mouth forming a wide smile.
"I can breathe now, I'm happy,
I can move my hands now, I'm happy!"
Happy for the small things,
Happy for the things we all take for granted,
Happy to be able to breathe.
Oh, Mother, what an act of courage!
What an example you set for your children,
For all the people who watch you
battling for your life.
What an example for the doomed people,
who believe cutting life short,

out of pain is something to desire.
Happy for the sacred gift of life.

Rea-Silvia Costin, P.E.© 2005

Author's Comments:
I wrote this poem a few years back and thought of it now, for Valentine Day!

Dear Mother,

Forgive me for not spending more time with you,
In your time of need,
In your time of fear,
In your time of doubting…

Did I understand you were at the death's gate?
Did I understand you were fighting for your life?
Did I understand your fear?
Did I understand your pain?

Mother; forgive me for not holding your hand
And reassuring you
Of the good things to come…

Mother forgive me for not sharing with you
My convictions, my beliefs,

That good and goodness is awaiting you,
That light is where you go, not dark;
No reason to be afraid!

Mother forgive me, please,
For my callousness.

Rea-Silvia Costin, P.E. © 2005

To Mother

"I've had those suits for twenty years,"
Mother said, pointing out to the neatly
hung suits, looking as new.
"How can anyone wear the same suits for twenty
years?" I was silently wondering,
a small girl looking up to my mother.
Now, the suits are still neatly hanging
in the closet.
My mother gone...Me... a grown woman.
Now, I dream of mother,
I dream of her every night,
wearing a big straw hat with a green ribbon,
a flowery, spring dress,
my mother young, her face smiling,
walking on a green pasture...
"She always liked hats,

she always liked walking," I was thinking,
"I'm so glad she's happy over there,
she doesn't have to wear the suits any longer."

Rea-Silvia Costin

Copyright ©2005 Rea-Silvia Costin

The Dash

A life span is a dash—
Between the time you were born
To the time your life ends
Here on earth.

A dash line represents
Your Life span
How well do you spend
Your time here on Earth?

What were your accomplishments?
Children?
Grandchildren?
A job well done?
Did you command
Respect from your peers?
Love from your family?

Did your example
Fire up people?

Did your words
Change people's lives,
or maybe improve just one life
For the better?

A dash line
Is a Life span.
How do you spend yours?

Rea-Silvia Costin, P.E. © 2005

Hold My Hand.

Lord, hold my hand
While I'm passing through the valley of shadows
That I'm not left alone
In my time of distress,
In my time of sorrows

Death and sorrow has clouded my days
Lord, hold my hand
While I'm passing through the valley of shadows.

Alone, I cannot bear it all
Lord, held my hand
While the sun
Clouds over the sky of my life

Rea-silva costin ©2002

Floating on the Wings of Love.

Floating on the wings of love
Climbing on the steps of clouds
Step after heavy step
Excruciating step after excruciating step
Reaching for the love eternal
Reaching for the light eternal

Climbing on the steps of clouds
Heavy step after heavy step
Reaching for the open arms
Waiting for me at the end of the stairway
To lighten up the heavy burden,
The unbearable pain,
Which tightens my heart
Squeezing it as a big fist

Floating on the wings of love
The eternal love which
Erases all pain

Of the poor, painful heart
Reaching for the open arms
At the end of the clouds' stairs.

Rea-Silvia Costin P.E.©2002

This poem is featured in the "Best Poems and Poets of 2005" collection of the International Library of Poetry.

I Cannot Say

To my brother, Radu

To the dearest people,
To my family,
To my closest friends,
Even to the one I love,
I cannot say, "I love you!"
What it is that keeps me from saying the simple words,
When the truth is that I love them more than I can say?
The true love, which withstands time
And obstacles, and hardships
The love that reunites us as a family,
As a whole, when the world seems to be against us,
The love which huddles us together,
Shoulder next to shoulder
And heart next to heart, as a wall,

When life's storms beat merciless against us
Why it is that I simply cannot say the words,
"I love you", the reassurance...
Why?

Rea-Silvia Costin, P.E.

Copyright ©2005 Rea-Silvia Costin, P.E.

Call Upon Christ to Enter Your Life

When the load you're carrying
is unbearably heavy
for your shoulders alone,
Call upon Christ to enter your life.

When crises at home are beyond your control,
when the family members claw at each other
for no reason at all,
Call upon Christ to enter your life.

When the greed and hate,
the jealousy and spite,
are taking over your life, destroying it,
Call upon Christ to enter your life.

When your home lies within total darkness,
when you are stumbling at night
not knowing which direction to go,
Let the light of Christ enter your life.

You could almost see it,
as if seeping through the cracks...
Let the light flood your home,
and the people inside!

Rea-Silvia Costin, P.E.©2005

I Chose You
(The Profession of Faith)

You did not choose Me, I Chose you
To do My work, to bear fruit for Me.
You did not choose Me,
I called upon you to carry on My work
To carry on My word, to put it in writing
For others to read and marvel.
I gave you the talent to put words together
To reach people's heart, to carry on My word.
I chose you,
To reach as many people as you can
With the power of your words,
The power, that I gave you
When you sit in front of your computer.
I chose you to do My work,
To spread the word of the gospel,
The eternal truth,
To as many people as you possibly can.
I chose you, don't give up!

It's not your work you're writing
It's My work, My words...Don't give up!

Rea-Silvia Costin, P.E.

Copyright ©2005 Rea-Silvia Costin

An Empty Vessel.

You are a vessel
An empty vessel
Ready to be filled out
With God's spirit
With the Holy Spirit

Your body is a temple
For the Holy Spirit
To dwell in

Prepare it thus
As a holy temple
Do not let sin
Smear the holy temple of God

When temptations
Are extending
Their leery hands
To take over your body
Like the multiple hands of an octopus
Ready to devour you

Resist it
And the devil will flee you
Keep the temple of God
Free of sin
Ready for the Holy Spirit
To dwell in it.

Rea-Silvia Costin©2002

The Tree next to the River's Waters

The tree next to the river's waters
Grows tall and green
Leafy, full of life.
It feeds on the river's waters,
It feeds on the river of life.

Like a person living close to God
Feeding on the waters of love,
Feeding on the waters of life,
The love of God,
Eternal, overwhelming love.
That person grows strong and generous,
His heart giving and caring,
Overflowing with love
Enough to feed other people,
Enough to give life
To less fortunate persons.

Feeding on the love of God
Like the tree next to the river's waters

That grows willowy branches
Feeding on the river's waters,
Feeding on the waters of life.

Rea-Silvia Costin, P.E. © 2005

Givers and Takers

God has created us in his image, Givers and Takers.
I'm a giver,
who thought it would be nice
to be on the receiving end sometimes.

Then, thought it better God has given me so much,
that from the abundance of His gifts to me,
I can give others.

Think of those who God gave nothing more,
than the crumbs from the giver's table.
Are they more fortunate than us?

We have God to give us plenty,
Those have only us to give them,
the leftovers of God's abundance.

Is it better to give, or to receive?

Rea-Silvia Costin, P.E. © 2005

Author's Comments:
This poem is also posted on my web site at poetry.com under my real name.

Flowing with the Flow of Waters

Flowing with the flow of waters
Carried upon the river's ripples,
Following Creator's plan,
Tailored just for me.
For so long,
I've swum against the river's current
Stubbornly trying to force my will,
Implementing my own plan.
Since I've learned to let go
Things that never seamed feasible,
Started falling into place
Like pieces of a puzzle
Moved by a giant hand.
My out of control life
Started to shape up
Just the way I've dreamed it
Flowing with the flow of waters
Following the Creator's plan.

Rea-Silvia Costin, P.E.©2002

Beauty

Beauty is just skin deep
We, human beings, are perishable species.
Our destiny here, on Earth,
Is to pass through life in a moment's time,
In an eye's blink.
The perishable form changes with time,
And the beauty fades,
As we are in this World, but not of this World.
The inner beauty,
The eternal love,
The Holy Spirit which fills our souls,
That's what shines
Through the soul's mirror,
The eyes.
It radiates from inside out
And transforms the most humble faces
Into timeless beauties.
Beauty is just skin deep.

Rea-Silvia Costin, P.E. ©2005

Guilt

Search my heart, Thou God
Open up my heart
For any blockages, sins
Anything wicked in my life's past.

If sin is to be found
In front of Thee, my God
I confess it,
It is mine.

It belongs to the past
I promise Thee, my God
Please, forgive my iniquities.

Wilt Thou have compassion on me,
Tread my inequities under Thy feet,
And throw them into the debt of my accusers,
Until there are no more.

I will meditate on Thy word
Day and night
I will prosper,

And blossom like a tree on
the river bank,

I will be transformed by the renewal of my mind
I will complete Thy forgiveness
And forgive all unrighteousness
And move on!

Rea-Silvia Costin, P.E. ©2005

God's Angels

Like a whisper of love,
Like a blanket of love,
God's Angels,
Going about
Their duties:
Soothing,
Healing,
Protecting,
Preventing.

Rea-Silvia Costin, P.E.©2005

The Inside Warrior

A flying eagle passed my window,
as I was still lying in bed, worrying sick,
over some insurmountable obstacle,
over not being able to climb it,
to step to the next plateau,
to live the more abundant life that I deserve.

Then I heard a sermon,
about not giving up Hope,
about not leaving any space for doubt
within yourself,
for the enemy to squeeze in,
the enemy that eats you up from inside out,
like a worm next to the apple's core.

And the thought formed clear within my mind:
"The war is fought from inside out!"
When no doubt is left within your soul
that you can climb the highest peak,

that you deserve the more abundant life,
Then the Victory is yours,
The reality will mirror the
Victory inside.

Change the Worrier for the Warrior
and start living the abundant life today!

Rea-Silvia Costin, P.E. ©2005

Author's Comments:
This poem was published in 2004 in "The International Who's Who in Poetry."

Measure of Success

"All the knowledge of this world is vanity,"
the wise King Solomon said.
As a person increases his knowledge,
He increases his sorrows,
For much grief comes of knowledge,
Much grief comes of understanding.

All the knowledge of this world,
All the wisdom of this world,
Does not bring
Happiness,
Joy,
Fulfillment,
Peace,
As the late King found toward his days' end.

All the pleasures of this world,
Which the wealthy King had indulged in
The love of wine,
Of many women, Of money,
The love of food,
All are vanity and vexation in the end.

Only God's blessings
Upon a person,
Only the Holy Spirit, which fills your being
Can ultimately fill the void in a person's heart,
In a person's soul,
Bringing him
Peace,
Joy,
Happiness.

Rea-Silvia Costin, P.E. ©2005

Terms of Endearment

As a groom, bent down on one knee
Asking his precious bride
To become his,

As a groom laying his love and his life
And all his earthly possessions
At the feet of his beloved,

As a groom presenting his bride
With a beautiful diamond ring
As a small token of his love to come,

For an endearment of his Commitment
To always cherish her, love her, take care of her
To provide for her

So is God giving us
Here, on earth,
A small token of his love

A token of His promises to be fulfilled
Of eternal life and love,
Of an abundant life

To live forever
In heaven,
In His very presence.

His token of love is the Holy Spirit
Filling our beings here, on earth
Bringing us peace.

It's just an endearment for the love to come
For the peace to come, the abundant life to come
For the light to come
Just as a small token indeed
That we are beholden
That we belong to Him.

Copyright©2005 Rea-Silvia Costin, P.E.

That which is Good.

That which is good,
That which I want to say
That I don't say.
That which is evil
That which I don't want to say
That I'm saying
How very true!
The old greatest wisdom
Coming straight from the mouth of the Apostles
How true it is
Even today, when I'm trying to build
A relationship
To open my soul to the one I love
To say what is in my mind and in my soul
All the beauty God has endowed me with
All the beauty hidden inside me
Trying to find its way out
To shine in the limelight.

How true it is!
That which is good and I want to say
That I don't say
That which is evil and I don't want to say
That I'm saying.

Rea-Silvia Costin, P.E. ©2005

War

How do you tell
a military man,
from Jacksonville, Florida,
who is preparing to go to war,
that his cause is not just?

How do you tell
his widow,
and his orphaned children,
that their father didn't fight a just war?

How do you explain
to the actors and actresses
in Los Angeles,
who demonstrated against war,
that their careers are in shambles?

How do you justify
to the mother in Iraq,
who is mourning her dead children,
that they were casualties of an unjust war?

How do you explain
to the Iraqi people,
whose historic buildings now lay in ruins,
and their ancient museums raped,
that the war was for their own good?

How do you explain all of this?
Only history will tell.

Rea-Silvia Costin, P.E.© 2003

Author's Comments:
This poem was included into "The Best Poems and Poets of 2003" and was awarded the Editors' Choice Award.

Jacksonville's Superbowl

to Jacksonville

The week of the superbowl,
the coronation of five years of hard work
for the City of Jacksonville, Florida.

It's cold and raining,
terrible weather
a fine mist, and the air cold, fog...

Our town will not show well
to the guests
Who want to go outside in such weather?

Cupped inside my office,
looking outside
from the 8th floor window
of the City Hall:
on the river side
there is this great ship that just anchored
next to the blue bridge,
the bridge that they just finished painting

a phosphorescent blue.
On the other side the Bay Street
(hoping to became the next Bourbon Street)
They set up huge, white tents
one next to another.

Cold, the wind is rushing
between the old, massive buildings
Even the TV anchormen looked sad
No one on the riverfront, or on the Bay Street
It's just Thursday
before the superbowl.

Friday, the sun braked through the dark clouds
It's still cold,
but with the sun shining on the blue sky,
who cares?
People started to crowd
on the river front,
on the Bay Street.

At lunchtime (mind you)
I stroll on the river walk
I drink in the blue sky, the crisp air
Smaller crafts, yachts,
anchored now along the river walk
in front of the Landing
as many as three, one next to the other
The Party is on!

I stroll by, drinking in the crowds
What is his name,
the actor that I saw in the movies,

coming out of the Adam's Mark hotel
driving a brand new Rolls Royce?

I stroll by, drinking in the City, the people
At the Landing there are so many people
I'm afraid they'll fall from the balconies
someone, a celebrity is interviewed,
or maybe there is the boobs' contest
(I saw it advertised from an airplane)

Saturday, before the superbowl
I have to get downtown,
I cannot drive,
I'll not be able to find a parking spot
I'll have to ride the skyway,
never done it before
even though it was built several years ago.
Crowds are waiting in line for the skyway
outsiders, visitors, of course,
the locals never take the skyway
I'll dare it this time
the ride is incredible
It crosses the river
It accelerates and decelerates
it bends and turns
What a view of the town
It's breathtaking!

The Bay street is lined with tents
the food is presented
on paper plates, up front
the Crispy Cream Trucks
rolling out fresh doughnuts

the bands singing on the huge stage

that was just built
the white lamps—balloons hanging from the wires
in the middle of the street
It is Bourbon Street
the Party is on!

Sunday of the superbowl
I do not have tickets,
nobody that I know has tickets
I'll watch the game at home
and toast it with a cold beer
What's the big deal about the superbowl anyhow?

Rea-Silvia Costin, P.E.©2005

Okefenokee Swamp

A milky mist is rising above marshes,
Like a fog forming.
The sun is up already,
but we cannot see its face for
the pine trees, reaching high.
A narrow path, one foot above swamp level,
is barely enough for the four-wheeler to pass.
Alligators reaching from the murky waters
with their mouths wide opened,
Snakes undulating their slick bodies,
mostly, inoffensive water moccasins.
A snow-white egret balancing graceful on one leg,
waiting our passage.
At a distance, a deer racing.
Quiet, only the sound of
alligators slithering through the muddy waters
Watching, waiting...

Rea-Silvia Costin, P.E. ©2005

Bird Feeder (Haiku)

Bird feeder: red and
Blue robins, doves, even squirrels
Cunning cat moves in.

Rea-Silvia Costin, P.E. ©2005

The Spin Class

To anyone who loves extreme sports!

One, two, three, four, Up!
One, two, three, four, Down!
From the corner of my eye, I watch
The big clock on the wall
It's been half an hour into class
Half to go One,

two, three, four, Up!
One, two, three, four, Down!
The sweat trickles from my forehead
Into my heavy mascara

One, two, three, four, Up!
One, two, three, four, Down!
The instructor calls at even intervals
My heart beats into my ears
My calves are aching

One, two, three, four, Up!
One, two, three, four, Down!
Through sweat and tears

I eye the clock on the wall
Five more minutes to go!
I can dream of lunch now!

Rea-Silvia Costin, P.E. ©2005

Hurricane Katrina.

Big, overcast eyes
Looking up, heavenly way,
On a shallow, brown face
Modest attire,
A bottle of coke half full
In hand, an oversized purse
Hanging over her shoulder,
"It's God will;
Only God can decide our fate now!"
Waiting patiently to be cleared
by security to enter the Dome
of New Orleans,
The last refuge, the only one,
For people like her
with no means of evacuating
In face of calamity
"I'd rather die here with my family
than come back later and bury them!
It's God will
I will pray!"
So her prayers along with thousands
Of others in the Dome,

And millions of others watching
The calamity approaching
Had a bearing on God's will.
The town ten feet below sea level
Was spared the full force of the hurricane
People inside the Dome were safe.
Others on the East Coast were not so lucky.
Houses toppled by flood,
Roads toppled by flood,
Cars toppled by water,
The wait just started.

Rea-Silvia Costin, P.E. ©2005

Hurricane Katrina-Part II

"The Town is Dead!"
The anchorman announced with teary eyes.
The town of light, Of fun and fancy carnivals,
Lying under two stories of water,
A cesspool, infested
With raw sewage and dead bodies.
The levees designed to protect the city,
Were designed on a budget,
Designed to fail.
One hundred thousand refugees;
Anyone care to shelter them?
Disoriented people, scared,
Waiting on the rooftops
To be rescued,
Looting, firearms at large,
Destitute people
Isn't time we face up to our responsibilities?

Rea-Silvia Costin, P.E. © 2005

Creativity

To the poets

Creativity is
Like a beam of light,
That reflects and
Deflects
As it touches us,
And increases
In size
And brightness
As it touches all of us.

Rea-Silvia Costin ©2005

My Favorite Hiding Place

My favored hiding place
From the worries of this world,
From the harsh realities,
From hurts that I can't cope with,

Sickness that I can't heal,
Problems that I can't solve,
Is this poetry site.

Once I've lost myself
In somebody else's fantasy,
Or work of imagination,
Or wallowed in somebody else's pain and suffering,
Sharing their emotions,
Partaking of their sorrows,
Their laughs and joys,
Touching their soul,
I've promptly forgot
All my worries of this world.

Rea-Silvia Costin, P.E. ©2005

The Game of Tagging

The game of tagging
It's new to me.
However, my friend
Neneng had tagged me
So I have to answer.

When I joined this site
(By sheer luck)
My spirit was down;
I was demoted
From a job
That I thought was my calling.

Boyfriends and former lovers
Have left me
For greener pastures
And fresher loves,
So, the first poem that
I posted on this site was one on Revenge!
Not many stars did I receive
My words of scorn were not well received!
The loved shared on this site

Healed my wounded heart,
And pride.

Words of love that I have
Long forgotten,
Buried in my memory's shelves Appeared in the light
And I put them on the paper.
For love shared is a powerful tool,
Creativity shared
Is a powerful tool,
In mending hearts
And creating better poetry.
Ruby Love, and crj147,
L. D. Harding, and Climingbird,
Eclect, and Godbreathed,
Brucerb, and grayfriar2003
Have changed my outlook in life
Therefore, here I'm tagging them.

Rea-Silvia Costin, P.E. © 2005

Author's comments: The Game of Tagging (as I found out) is to recognize and prompt other poet(s) whose work had impressed upon you, to respond in kind.

As I Read Your Poem

To all poets at poets.com site.

As I read your poem,
I could feel your sadness
within my heart,
I could feel your tears
In my eyes.

As I read your poem,
My lips smiled with you,
I laughed with you,
Not at you.

As I read your poem,
I could feel your pain,
The harsh words
Were thrown at me too.

As I read your poem,
Your loss became mine,

Your desolation
Became mine.

As I read your poem,
I've shared the love
You hold so dear,
I too was transported
In a fairytale world.

As I read your poem,
I too visited
The lush, green forest,
I too could hear
The birds' songs.

As I read your poem,
I've become you.

Rea-Silvia Costin, P.E. @2005

Spring

Spring is the time of love
For love blooms in the spring of life
It's springtime again

Flowers are blooming
The air is full of their perfume
Spring is the time for love

The spring of my life has passed
Outside it's springtime
And love is blooming in the spring of life

Oh! How I long for love again
For spring is the time for love
And birds are singing

When will my heart sing again
In harmony with nature?
For love is blooming in the springtime

The spring of my life has passed
But my heart is young
And longing for love again
For Love is blooming in the springtime.

Rea-Silvia Costin, P.E. © 2002

The Most Precious Stone.

Among all precious stones
Shining bright in their beauty,
The stone of Love,
Faith,
Goodness
There is an ugly stone
That none of us want to see
The ugly stone of
Pain,
Long Suffering,
Death
The ugly stone
Of
Calvary Suffering
That none of us wants to see
And all of us have seen
The ugly stone
We so much fear seeing
It has its inner beauty
Should you bother to look
Beyond its ugly face
It has the inner beauty

Of
Strength building,
And long suffering
It has the inner beauty
Of
Character building,
Helping us become better Christians,
More in the image of our Creator
It has the inner beauty
Of
Godly touch
Upon our souls

The ugly stone
Shines brighter amongst all precious stones
Should you bother to look beyond its ugly face
More precious indeed.

Rea-Silvia Costin, P.E. ©2005

Thoughts

Thoughts are the foundation of things to come,
As real as any material things.
Thoughts are invisible waves crossing space
To reach the Almighty God, the Creator,
For all good things come from God,
Every pure and just thing comes from God.
Thoughts are forms of energy,
Impulses sent by you into space,
Wishes of happiness and fulfillment,
Wishes for good health, and healing,
Wished for material things;
They reach God and reverberate back to you,
In material forms,
Or the accomplishment of the innermost desires.
Good thoughts, Happy endings
They're all in God's hands
But they generate from your thoughts.

Rea-Silvia Costin, P.E. © 2005

We Are Who We Became

First, we are who God intended us to be
If we would let God be our lives' Guide
We have an Agreement with God, each one of us,
Made even before we're born.

Second, we are who we became
Through affiliations with families, friends,
Culture and society's rules,
If we allow them to take our life's control.

Third, we are what we allow ourselves to be:
A smiling face, radiating goodness, love,
Or a prune face,
Radiating hate and resentment.

Have you met people
Whose company you seek, whose love warms your life?
And others that you rather not be around?
It's all about each person's outlook on life!

Ultimately, it's as they say:
"The aging of your face
Reflects who you are inside!"
Who would you rather be?

Rea-Silvia Costin, P.E.© 2005

Vengeance

Oh God, turn thy face away
from my adversaries,
who sap my life,
my energy, and my blood!

Oh God, thine is the vengeance
in thee I trust
to avenge me of my adversaries,
who took away my youth,
and my innocence,
my work, and my love!

Oh God, thine is the vengeance
avenge me of my adversaries,
who used my work and my love
to wipe their dirty feet
before entering
a more lucrative business,
a more desirable love.

Oh God, thine is the vengeance
I saw it working before,
doing its justice,
in front of my very eyes,
like a dream that I had already dreamed.

Oh God, thine is the vengeance
Avenge me!

Rea-Silvia Costin © 2005

Birthday Presents

"I sent the last ray of the day
To cast a glitter on the golden chain lying
Down on the ground, for her to see !"
The Angel muttered.
"It's my birthday again!
For all the care I'm giving others
None will give me a present!
Not that I need anything,
A golden chain would be nice though!
I'll park my car over here.
Oh! Look what I just found:
A golden chain!
Exactly what I wanted for my birthday!"

"Pure coincidence," the skeptic will say,
But I know better,
For this year, a few days before my birthday
A golden ring I found

Next to a trashcan on the street!
Coincidence, or do I get my gifts from above?
I'd like to think the later!

Rea-Silvia Costin, P.e. ©2005

The Pruning

I was told the vine,
becomes more vigorous
when it's pruned.
It's cut way back,
the dead branches and a little bit more
of the live ones,
to prepare it for the new growth...

God is preparing us for better work,
The cut is bleeding, the pain is excruciating
It needs to be done for the new branches
to bear fruit, much fruit...

Do we have a choice?
Do we have a say?
People and relationships,
houses and native land,
all earthly possessions,
loved ones,
have been cut mercilessly away from me
the dead ones, and a little bit more...

Every time He pruned me,
did I fulfill the promise?
Every time I bled,
did I fulfill the promise?

Rea-Silvia Costin, P.E. ©2005

Undying Love

"Jesus Christ really loves you!"
the young girl muttered.
Mouth gaped open,
fireworks inside me,
I looked dumbfounded at the girl passing by.
Does she know something I don't know?
Is there a sign on my forehead that states:
I belong to the Lord?
"What a wonderful thought," I replied,
the heavy burden from my shoulders lifting
the doom from my heart replaced with joy.
"That's the truth," she replied,
and serenely walked away.
A random encounter?
Then why has it changed my entire outlook?
Why has it touched my soul so deeply?
Perhaps it is the Lord's way
of reassuring me of his undying love.

Rea-Silvia Costin, P.E. ©2005

Author's Comments: This poem was published in the "Throwing Stardust" collection of the International Library of Poetry and was recorded on the "Sound of Poetry collection."

Have You Ever Wondered?

Have you ever wondered
when you are at a crossroads in your life,
when you are in greatest need for advice,
when your heart is heavy,
when your chest is aching,
when your head is pounding,
when tears are running down your cheeks
and you haven't even noticed them... Have you wondered
how it happens that when you opened your eyes
when you opened your ears
you could hear God's personal message to you
on the radio, or on television, or by the word
of total strangers, or in a dream...
The word of God comes directly to you
when you are in need
just open your eyes,

just open your ears
listen carefully
God is near, comforting you...

Rea-Silvia Costin, P.E.© 2005

This poem has been published on the Eternal Portraits Anthology published by the International Library of Poets in 2005.

Redemption

Redemption
In a religion of sin
And accusations,
Of darkened soul
The lightened image of our Savior,
Hope and salvation
No more accusations,
But joy.

Rea-Silvia Costin, P.E. ©2005

www.ingramcontent.com/pod-product-compliance
Lightning Source LLC
Chambersburg PA
CBHW050528160726
48003CB00002B/503